A Tiger Roars:

The Story of Jhoon Rhee, Martial Arts Legend

Michael Shackelford

Designed by Rocket Pop Media

Edited by Tammy Shackelford

Arlington, Virginia • 2018

Table of Contents

Linda Lee Cadwell

My dear friend Grandmaster Jhoon Rhee,

Congratulations on the 50th anniversary of the Jhoon Rhee Institute. You are living proof of how great a difference one person's life can make to millions around the world. Your friend, Bruce Lee, would be proud of your myriad of accomplishments since those beginning days when the two of you talked at length about the future of martial arts. You have turned that future into reality as your messages of truth, beauty and love have helped so many to find happiness in their lives.

Not only have you been on the world's stage for more than five decades, but you have also been a kind and loving personal friend for the nearly 50 years I have known you. From the times our families spent hours in each other's living rooms discussing every aspect of life to the days after Bruce passed away, you have been a pillar of support and love in my life. You are an international treasure to the world; to me, you are someone I know I can always count on. Bruce would be ever so grateful for your care and concern for his family over all the years.

Bask in the joy of your success in having established an institute that for 50 years has excelled in producing qualified martial artists who themselves go forth and lead by your example. I know your work will never be done as long as there is one more person who needs to hear your message of strength and happiness. As Bruce used to say, "Walk On! My friend."

With love and respect,

Linda

1

A Tiger Roars (1931 - 1945)

In a luxurious palace, somewhere in Korea, a young woman hears the roar of a tiger, thundering from the darkness of the surrounding jungle. She's not afraid, because the palace is protected by a high and heavy wall. But the roar is deafening. It startles her—and she wakes up.

The palace, the wall, the tiger—it was all a dream. But it was a very special kind of dream, what Koreans call a taemong, or conception dream. The woman was Kay Im Rhee, the year was 1931, and her first son, Jhoon Rhee, was on the way.

Years later, thinking back on his mother's taemong, Jhoon Rhee described what he believes the dream meant. "I think it has to do with the prominence I've been lucky to achieve with my Tae Kwon Do activities—the 'noise' I've made throughout the world outside my mother's castle: Korea."

Jhoon Rhee in "When Tae Kwon Do Strikes"

Nine months after his mother's taemong, on January 7, 1932, Jhoon Rhee was born in the small Korean village of Sanyangri, Asan. His father, Jinhoon, was a clerk in a small business. His mother was a housewife. The couple already had two daughters, but as the first son, Jhoon Rhee was an especially welcome baby; at that time in Korea, most parents preferred to have boys. Eventually, the couple would have a total of five children.

Despite this auspicious beginning, there were few signs of the roaring tiger to come. While still an infant, Rhee was accidentally dropped by his ordinarily very careful 7-year-old sister, and his thigh bone was broken. On that same day, Rhee's maternal grandfather died. Following an old Korean belief, Rhee's mother carried her baby son five miles so that she could place her dead father's hand on Rhee's broken leg. The fracture healed soon after.

Because of the accident, Rhee's family believed he would never be athletic, and as a child he was indeed smaller and a slower runner than his peers. Rhee, however, was determined to compensate for his size and speed, so he decided at a young age—before even turning five—to study martial arts. He couldn't begin immediately, though; there were no martial arts schools near Rhee's home. In the meantime, Rhee resolved to begin lifting weights and build his strength.

Rhee's weight-building program began in earnest when he was six. He had recently returned to his village after spending a year living with his paternal grandfather and uncle—an "exchange program" meant to teach children independence, especially from their mother. Back in his village, Rhee came home from school one day crying. When his mother asked what was wrong, Rhee explained that a tough five-year-old neighbor girl had slapped him. Rhee says that his mother was appalled that he had let himself be assaulted by a girl—especially a younger girl. To raise his self-confidence, Rhee committed himself to weight training with renewed focus, and continued training until he was 13, when he moved to Seoul to enroll in Dong Sung High School.

Jhoon Rhee's father, Jin Hoon Rhee (1909-1960)

Jhoon Rhee's mother, Kay Im Rhee (1906 - 1994)

Rhee's notion of self-improvement, even at this young age, wasn't limited to physical strength. After starting high school, he began teaching himself violin, learning to play Korean folk songs by ear. His love of the violin, as well as the harmonica, was part of an appreciation for music and the arts that would carry through his whole life, and eventually even become part of his approach to Tae Kwon Do.

As Rhee entered his teens, he was becoming stronger and more confident—a few steps closer to the roaring tiger of his mother's dream. But it wasn't only Rhee who was changing; his country was changing, too. In the summer of Rhee's 14th year, on August 15, 1945, Korea gained its independence from Japanese colonial rule. Rhee says that he was too young at the time to understand the event's full significance; it wasn't until later that the idea of freedom from domination became truly meaningful for him, when the North and South of his country went to war in 1950.

CHAPTER TWO

Dreaming of America (1945 - 1950)

For the Rhee family, the years after World War II felt like a return to normal life. Still, there were differences, and for the teenaged Rhee, one of the most exciting changes was that Korean martial arts could now be taught openly.

During Japanese colonial rule, traditional Korean martial arts, like almost all aspects of Korean identity, had been banned. When the occupation ended in 1945, Korean martial arts schools began to open. The first of these schools was founded by Grandmaster Won Kook Lee, and the style that he taught, though based on traditional Korean martial arts, was something new. Eventually called Tae Kwon Do, the new style incorporated various influences, combining combat techniques, self-defense, sport, and exercise.

Chung Do Kwon students.
Jhoon Rhee (5th seated on ground) 1946

With the opening of these schools, Jhoon Rhee was finally able to achieve his longtime goal of studying martial arts. In 1947, when Rhee was 15, he enrolled in Chung Do Kwan, Grandmaster Won Kook Lee's Tae Kwon Do academy in Seoul. For the first three months, Rhee didn't tell his father that he had enrolled—although Korean martial arts could be studied openly again, martial arts in general had a very poor reputation and were considered little better than street fighting.

When Rhee's father came to visit his son in Seoul, he was upset to discover that Rhee was studying Tae Kwon Do, but he was persuaded by Rhee's uncle to allow the teenager to continue training

Another exciting change for Rhee, now that the Japanese occupation had ended, was up on the big screen: American movies were being shown in local theatres. Rhee had to sneak in, at first, because high schoolers weren't allowed to buy tickets. Rhee says he was captivated by the beautiful American actresses—especially the blondes. In fact, he was so taken with the images on the screen that he set himself a new goal: he would some day marry a blonde. The only problem with this decision, as Rhee saw it, was that there were no blondes in Korea. So he resolved, as he sat there in the darkened theatre, that he would eventually move to America.

But how, Rhee wondered, could he make a living in a whole different country? How could he support a family? The answer, Rhee realized, lay in the martial arts training he had waited so long to begin. He would introduce Tae Kwon Do to America and earn his living there as an instructor.

With his new dream in place, Rhee immediately began to study English with intense determination, and he was soon recognized by teachers and classmates alike as his school's most advanced English student. Almost no one knew that he was studying Tae Kwon Do just as hard.

Meanwhile, Rhee's small size continued to make him a target for bullies. By the eleventh grade, he had earned his brown belt in Tae Kwon Do, but few of his classmates knew about his training, and he was still picked on constantly. That all changed when, one day at school, a notorious bully grabbed a pencil out of Rhee's hand and was rude when Rhee asked for its return. Rhee decided it was time to put his training to the test. He told the bully that they should meet after classes.

Rhee was nervous as the hour of the meeting approached—he wondered if his training would allow him to defend himself in an actual confrontation. The bully arrived and wasted no time starting the fight. He swung at Rhee first, but Rhee quickly countered, punching the boy in the eye and kicking him in the throat. Muttering "you got me," the bully immediately gave up.

At school the next day, when the bully showed up with a black eye, word of the fight quickly spread. Rhee was suddenly seen in a different light—no longer was he the little kid, the target, a victim picked on by bullies. Now he was respected. And with that respect, Rhee's confidence grew. His dream of teaching Tae Kwon Do in America felt like something he could actually achieve. His next step was college; he had been accepted at Dong Kook University after graduating high school in 1950.

But Rhee's life, and the life of his country, was about to take a turn.

CHAPTER THREE

A Country at War (1950 - 1953)

Rhee was barely settled at Dong Kook University when the Korean War broke out on June 25, 1950. Instead of pursuing his studies and advancing his dream to teach Tae Kwon Do in America, Rhee found himself fleeing south with his nine-year-old brother, to be with their grandfather.

Around July 4, only a few days before North Korean Communist troops passed through the area, Rhee and his brother reached their grandfather's home, where they stayed for a month. Despite the danger, they then decided to head for their home in Suwon, because their mother was there alone.

Although only 90 miles away, the journey took three days because Rhee and his brother had to travel on foot. They regularly had to hide from air attacks, but were helped along the way by friendly strangers who took them in and fed them.

Jhoon Rhee with fellow soldiers

Rhee and his brother reached their mother safely, but the reunion was brief. By August, Rhee had to go underground—literally. Since Rhee was 18 years old, if he were discovered staying with his mother, he would have been forced to register and would sooner or later have been drafted into the North Korean Army. So, for two months, Rhee lived in a cellar, until the Americans landed and pushed the Communist army north beyond Pyongyang. On September 28, 1950, Rhee emerged, ready to fight for his country alongside the Americans.

By November, Rhee had joined a unit of the U.S. Air Force as an interpreter, putting his English skills to use in a way he had never expected. Over the course of the next year, Rhee continued to work as an interpreter for both the Americans and the British, until he was drafted into the South Korean Army and began his service in the 101st Battalion.

Conditions in the Battalion were severe, in part because corruption was rampant— Rhee's commanding officer, for instance, would keep most of the troops' food and supplies for himself and his friends, and in order to sell on the black market. When the Battalion was newly formed in Chulwon, near the front line, it was bitterly cold, but the troops lived in field tents with no heat and with only one blanket per person. Their meals consisted of three spoons of rice plus a couple of sips of salt water, and they were allowed to sleep no more than three or four hours a night.

Hundreds of thousands of South Koreans fled south in mid-1950 after the North Korean army invaded.

Hoping for a transfer out of the Battalion, Rhee decided to apply to officer cadet training school. It was not an easy decision to make, despite his current harsh circumstances: the casualty rate in the cadet officer corps was over 70%. Rhee fully expected that, if he were accepted into the corps, he would not survive. Still, Rhee felt that anything would be better than the hunger and cold in the Battalion.

After Rhee was accepted into the training school, his family shared the belief that his death was imminent. To relieve their fears, Rhee lied and told them that one of the officers in the program planned to keep Rhee at the school as a Tae Kwon Do instructor after his cadet training was complete.

Having comforted his family, Rhee resigned himself to his fate as his training neared its end. Then, on July 27, 1953, with Rhee's deployment only days away, the truce was declared. The war was over. All of the 250 cadets in Rhee's class believed they had been spared certain death.

Rhee says it felt like a miracle. He was alive. And his dream was still alive, too. Maybe he really could teach Tae Kwon Do in America some day.

Gary Air Force Base, circa 1953

CHAPTER FOUR

America at Last (1953 - 1957)

Now an officer, and with a new lease on life, Rhee applied for army aviation training. He soon switched his focus to weather and aircraft maintenance, and after his training was complete, he was assigned to teach others.

A year and a half into Rhee's instructor assignment, he heard about an opportunity for officers to train in aircraft maintenance in the United States. Here, Rhee hoped, was a chance to make his dream come true. He applied for the program, along with about 50 other officers. Only three would be accepted. Once again, Rhee's proficiency in English served him well. He passed the test with the highest grade. He was going to America.

Rhee landed in San Francisco in early June of 1956. The flight had been his first time in a plane, and Rhee says that when he first took his seat, he pinched his own cheek to make sure it wasn't a dream. The feeling of unreality became even more pronounced after his arrival. Rhee later recalled that he was completely unprepared for the splendor of the U.S.—the cars, the skyscrapers, the wealth of post-war America. He was particularly taken with the abundance of neon signs. And yes, the women were indeed beautiful, just as they were in the movies he had seen in Korea.

Jhoon Rhee, 1955

He was only in San Francisco for a day before flying to Austin, Texas, and then traveling by bus to Gary Air Force Base in San Marcos. As different as this new country was, Rhee found base routine familiar because of his military experience. He was the only Asian for miles around, but he felt welcomed and respected as an officer in a foreign army.

Rhee knew that his stay in America would only be temporary, limited to the length of the training program, but while he was in the U.S. he was determined to see if he had any chance of returning for good some day. He joined the local Methodist Church and made many new friends; over time, he let them know about his wish to stay and study in America. His new friends were supportive and eager to help, but in order to remain in America, Rhee would need an official sponsor. This was a significant responsibility—the sponsor would not only have to vouch for Rhee's character, but promise to support him financially if necessary.

As Rhee's time in the training program ran out, no sponsor had been found, so it was with a heavy heart that he attended church on the last Sunday before returning to Korea. During the service, however, the pastor made one final plea, asking the congregation if anyone was willing to take on the responsibility of sponsorship. To Rhee's surprise, an elderly couple, Mr. and Mr. Robert L. Bunting, agreed.

Jhoon Rhee's sponsors to the United States, Mr. & Mrs. Robert L. Bunting

High school alumni after the Korean War

朝鮮大學校第二部（軍人大學）學生一同 4288. 7. 20.

Chosun University, Kwan Joo

11

CHAPTER FIVE

The Dream Comes True (1957 - 1962)

Before beginning his new life in America, Rhee had to finish one last year in his term of enlistment in the South Korean Army. It was a long twelve months for Rhee, but by November of 1957, he had received his honorable discharge and was flying back to the U.S. When he landed, he had only forty-six dollars in his pocket.

By February of 1958, Rhee had enrolled at San Marcos Southwest State College. Two years later, he transferred to the University of Texas in Austin to study engineering. His plan was to finish his degree there in three years, but in the summer of 1962, he was given an unexpected opportunity—he was offered a job teaching in a karate school in Washington, DC.

Female Martial Arts Students - San Marcos (Professor Clara Gamble - tallest)

His dream was actually coming true. He was living in America, and about to begin teaching martial arts as his profession. However, when he arrived at the DC school, he discovered that there were only six students. Enrollment was so low, in fact, that the school could not even afford to pay Rhee.

Rhee decided to take a bold step. He would open his own martial arts studio. On June 28, 1962, he did exactly that, founding the very first Jhoon Rhee School of Tae Kwon Do at 2035 K Street NW, Washington, DC.

Class at the first Jhoon Rhee Institute at 2035 K. Street with students John St. Peter, John Kent, Richard Wood, McMahon

Jhoon Rhee at 2035 K. Street location in Washington, D.C., 1962

CHAPTER SIX

Expansion and Innovation (1962 - 1972)

Rhee wasted no time getting his new school off the ground. First, he wrote letters to many of the ambassadors from around the world who were serving in DC, telling them about the opening of his school. He promised that he could not only teach their children Tae Kwon Do, but also guarantee their children's character education and help them all make A's and B's in their academic studies.

Rhee also ran two small ads in the sports section of the Washington Post. He couldn't believe it when the phone rang all day with people asking for more information about tuition and class times.

Rhee's First Student - Richard Wood

On opening day, more than 200 people came to Rhee's small studio—less than 1,000 square feet—to see his one-man Tae Kwon Do demonstrations. The guest of honor was His Excellency, Ambassador Il-Kwon Chung of the South Korean Embassy. By the end of that first day, 12 people signed up for classes. Within a month, Rhee had more than 30 students. And by August, enrollment was over 125. Rhee never did return to the University of Texas to complete his studies, though he was later awarded an honorary doctorate from Seoul University. Instead, he focused his energies on growing his school and adding new ones.

Jhoon Rhee in his office at 2000 L. Street in Washington, D.C.

*Student Jose Jones and fellow student at 2000
L. Street location in Washington, D.C.*

*Instructor Bruce Turner with Jhoon Rhee at
the 1801 Connecticut Ave. location
in Washington, D.C.*

Instructor Ken Crawford

Dr. John G. Glowers, President, San Marcos South-west State Teachers College visits K street location

Group Student Picture, 2035 K Street location

Jhoon Rhee with his children Chun and Meme

As a way to reach new students, Rhee began running TV ads in the DC area, becoming the first Tae Kwon Do master to promote martial arts through television advertising. The commercials featured the slogan, "Nobody Bothers Me," and had a huge impact—at least on Rhee's three-year-old son, Chun. In the Rhee household, Chun began responding to the TV with the rejoinder, "Nobody bothers me, either." Eventually, Chun and his sister Meme appeared in a version of the commercial themselves. At the end of the TV spot, Meme intoned the original slogan, followed by Chun's "Nobody bothers me, either" and a quick wink. The commercial was so memorable and so appealing that its fame spread beyond the DC area and has been popular for decades since, thanks in part to its long presence on YouTube.

Meanwhile, in his schools, Rhee began to adapt and modify his approach to martial arts, rather than simply teach traditional Tae Kwon Do. This was in part due to the influence of Bruce Lee, who was a friend and colleague of Rhee's from 1964 until Lee's death in 1973. Lee convinced Rhee that blindly following tradition leads to stagnation in martial arts. To this day, Rhee respects the traditional approach, but he does not believe there is any single best style, not his own or anyone else's. Rhee says that, for him, the most important thing is to bring the benefits of martial arts and fitness to as many people as possible, and he believes there are many paths.

Rhee's relationship with Bruce Lee began in August of 1964, when they met at the late Grandmaster Ed Parker's International Karate Championships in Long Beach, California. Rhee was 32 years old; Lee, 23. Both men performed demonstrations, and each was impressed with the other's skill. They started a friendship, regularly visiting each other and exchanging letters for nearly a decade. Lee also attended the Jhoon Rhee Nationals every year from 1966 to 1970.

Jhoon Rhee with close friend, Bruce Lee, 1971

Photo session with Bruce Lee, 1972, ™ & © *Bruce Lee Enterprises, LLC. All Rights Reserved.*

Linda Lee Caldwell, Bruce Lee's widow, says, "Bruce had great respect for Jhoon Rhee's martial arts and the way he ran his schools. He always considered Jhoon quite a groundbreaker in putting on these highly regarded tournaments. They shared a goal of wanting to expose the American public to real martial arts—more than just the kicking and punching—the discipline and the underlying philosophy."

Photo session with Bruce Lee, 1972, ™ & © *Bruce Lee Enterprises, LLC. All Rights Reserved.*

Bruce Lee was not the only high-profile person to come into Rhee's circle around this time. In April of 1965, Rhee read a newspaper account of how Rep. James Cleveland of New Hampshire had been mugged and injured near Capitol Hill. Rhee immediately called Cleveland's office to say that he had a Tae Kwon Do school in DC and would like to teach the representative martial arts. When Cleveland called back the next day, asking about schedule and tuition, Rhee offered to teach him for free, even saying he would go to the Hill to save the representative's valuable time. Cleveland appreciated the offer so much that he told Rhee he would ask a few of his colleagues if they might also be interested in training, so that they could form a class on the Hill. And so began Rhee's U.S. Congressional Tae Kwon Do Club.

Senator Milton Young (1945 - 1981) & Senator Hiram Fong (HI) (1955 - 1977) Arm Wrestling

Jhoon Rhee Congressional Class with students Richard Ichord, Tom Beville, James Symington, Floyd Spence

The Club's first class was held in the House members' gymnasium on May 6, 1965; one of the first students, along with Rep. Cleveland, was Vice President Joe Biden. Since then, more than 350 members of Congress have attended classes—19 even earned black belts.

Over the years, the U.S. Congressional Tae Kwon Do Club has made national news on several occasions. One of the most widely covered events was a tournament organized by Rhee on September 14, 1975, featuring Republican vs. Democrat sparring matches. Aired on national television and also reported by the foreign press, the event was held in the DC Armory before a live audience of more than 5,000 people. The matches ended in a draw.

Of course, Rhee's expanding influence wasn't felt only in the political world. Throughout the 60s, his importance in the martial arts community continued to grow. For instance, Rhee played a seminal role in the career of Joe Lewis, well-known American kickboxer, point karate fighter, and actor who was twice voted the greatest fighter in karate history. While still in the Marine Corps and already an accomplished martial artist, Lewis was very much against the idea of tournament competition, believing that students in most karate schools did not train very hard. Still, in May 1966, Lewis decided to check out

Jhoon Rhee with Sportscaster Jim Simpson

Jhoon Rhee hosting Jhoon Rhee National Tournament with guest Bruce Lee, 1971

Jhoon Rhee National Championship Tournament televised on NBC Sports, 1971

22

Jhoon Rhee's National Championships. He had no plans to compete, but Rhee and Bruce Lee managed to convince him. Lewis later said, "Jhoon Rhee, who I respect a lot, was the man who started my fighting career by talking me into the competition."

Although Rhee believed strongly in the value of tournaments and competition, he was concerned that so much of Tae Kwon Do, at least overtly, revolved around violence. Rhee did not consider himself a violent man, and his attraction to Tae Kwon Do always had as much to do with philosophy as with action; in fact, Rhee has long said that martial arts without philosophy is simply street fighting.

Rhee continued to think about these issues through the late 60s, and decided to create something new with Tae Kwon Do that could balance the scales.

Jhoon Rhee National Tournament in Washington, D.C. Pictured Allen Steen and Ed. Parker (Judge)

Winner of the Jhoon Rhee National's tournament in Washington, D.C., Mike Stone, 1965

As a lover of dance and music, and someone who believed that the human form is the greatest of all works of art, Rhee wondered what it would be like to add music to the choreographed body movements of Tae Kwon Do, similar to the way that music is used in Olympic skating, ballroom dancing, and gymnastic floor exercise routines. Rhee choreographed several dances in ballet style, based on Tae Kwon Do moves, and set them to classical music, including Beethoven's Fifth Symphony and the theme from Exodus. The result of Rhee's invention—martial arts ballet—became the foundation for the musical forms competitions that are now popular at many martial arts tournaments in the U.S. The new art form has also found its way to Europe and Russia.

Rhee's concerns about violence in Tae Kwon Do also led him to invent safety equipment specifically designed for martial arts. One incident in particular motivated Rhee; at a 1969 championship tournament, he saw one of his students take a hard kick in the face, breaking his cheekbone. Rhee became determined to do something to reduce the frequency and severity of martial-arts-related injuries. The result was Jhoon Rhee Safe-T equipment, protective gear that covers the "weapons"—the hands and feet—and the head, allowing full-contact training and competition without the risk of serious injury. No one in martial arts had worn safety gear before Rhee invented it; he believes its presence has changed the nature of martial arts for the better, removing the stigma of brutality and attracting more women and children as students.

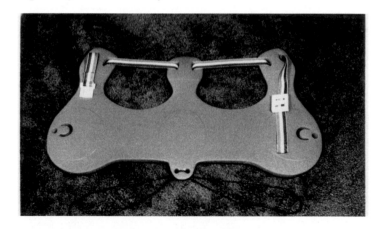

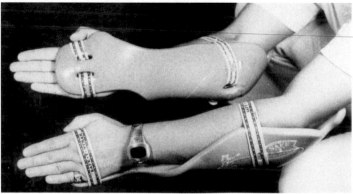

United States Patent

Des. 238,121
Patented Dec. 23, 1975

238,121
PROTECTIVE HELMET OR THE LIKE

Jhoon Goo Rhee, 2525 N. Ridgeview Road,
Arlington, Va. 22207

Filed Nov. 27, 1974, Ser. No. 527,904

Term of patent 14 years

Int. Cl. D2—03
U.S. Cl. D2—232

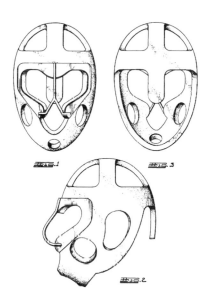

FIG. 1 is a front elevational view of a protective helmet showing my new design;
FIG. 2 is a side elevational view thereof; and
FIG. 3 is a rear elevational view.
I claim:
The ornamental design for a protective helmet or the like, as shown.

References Cited

UNITED STATES PATENTS

D. 190,716	6/1961	McMillan	D2—233
D. 217,894	6/1970	Mikita	D2—231
3,594,815	7/1971	Reese	2—3 R

LOIS S. LANIER, Primary Examiner

United States Patent [19]

Rhee

[11] **3,949,493**

[45] **Apr. 13, 1976**

[54] **PROTECTIVE SHOE**

[76] Inventor: **Jhoon Goo Rhee**, 2525 N. Ridgeview Road, Arlington, Va. 22207

[22] Filed: **Aug. 4, 1975**

[21] Appl. No.: **601,440**

[52] U.S. Cl. .... **36/2 R**
[51] Int. Cl.² **A41D 17/00**
[58] Field of Search .... 36/2 R, 7.1 R, 7.3, 2.5 R, 36/1.5, 2 A, 2 B, 8.1

[56] **References Cited**
UNITED STATES PATENTS

2,541,738	2/1951	Bassichis	36/8.1
2,657,477	11/1953	Winslow	36/2 R
2,814,887	12/1957	Hockley	36/2.5 A
3,769,722	11/1973	Rhee	36/2 R

Primary Examiner—Patrick D. Lawson
Attorney, Agent, or Firm—Millen, Raptes & White

[57] **ABSTRACT**

The invention relates to a protective shoe adapted to protect the foot of the wearer thereof engaging in the arts of karate, kung fu, etc. The shoe comprises a casing containing an energy-absorbent soft resilient material substantially open at the bottom. A retaining means on the open bottom is provided for aiding in the retention of the shoe on the foot of the wearer. Straps are also provided for aiding in the retention and for tightening the shoe on the foot of the wearer.

6 Claims, 3 Drawing Figures

United States Patent [19]

Rhee

[11] **Patent Number:** **4,635,300**

[45] **Date of Patent:** **Jan. 13, 1987**

[54] **KARATE GLOVE**

[76] Inventor: **Jhoon G. Rhee**, 6210 Chillum Pl., NW., Washington, D.C. 20011

[21] Appl. No.: **714,395**

[22] Filed: **Mar. 21, 1985**

[51] Int. Cl.⁴ **A41D 13/10**
[52] U.S. Cl. .... **2/16; 2/18; 2/161 A**
[58] Field of Search .... 2/16, 161 A, 18

[56] **References Cited**
U.S. PATENT DOCUMENTS

3,903,546	9/1975	Rhee	2/16
3,924,272	12/1975	Alen et al.	2/16
3,945,045	3/1976	Rhee	2/16
4,062,073	12/1977	Rhee	2/16
4,287,610	9/1981	Rhee	2/18
4,290,147	9/1981	Brückner et al.	2/161 A

FOREIGN PATENT DOCUMENTS

| 0054949 | 6/1982 | European Pat. Off. | 2/16 |

Primary Examiner—Louis K. Rimrodt
Attorney, Agent, or Firm—James C. Wray

[57] **ABSTRACT**

A unitary flexible protective glove molded of a resilient material and adapted to be easily worn on the hand for use in the art of karate and the like is disclosed. The glove, when worn, covers a portion of the lower forearm, the wrist, and the hand. The portion of the glove covering the wrist and hand is substantially tubular in shape and designed to wrap around the wrist and forearm without the need of any securing means. There is a thumb pocket having on the inside a restraining strap. There is also a grip loop for the index, middle, ring and little fingers which is in close proximity to a finger padding section. The finger padding section and grip loop are held in close proximity by a bridging strap. The glove is designed to facilitate easy insertion of the hand without the need of securing straps.

5 Claims, 5 Drawing Figures

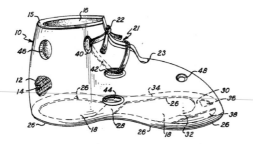

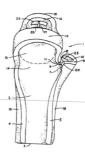

Won Kook Lee congratulating students after a belt promotion

As the 60s came to an end, Rhee was also working on a five-volume series of Tae Kwon Do books, which was eventually published and has been available to the public since 1970. By 1970, he was operating eight Jhoon Rhee Schools in the DC area, and even had studios in the Dominican Republic. His yearly Tae Kwon Do tournaments continued to grow in attendance and influence. Rhee's dream had come true beyond his wildest imaginings. But greater heights were still to come.

Student Mike Anderson opened a Jhoon Rhee Institute in Germany while stationed there (performsing jump kick)

Left to Right - Mother, Kay Im, Jhoon Rhee, Won Kook Lee (founder of Chung Do Kwon), and late wife Han Soon Rhee

27

CHAPTER SEVEN

Rising Fame (1972 - 1980)

Given the role that movies played in forming the teenaged Rhee's dream to eventually live in America and teach Tae Kwon Do, it seems only fitting that Rhee would himself star in a movie one day. In 1972, Bruce Lee wrote Rhee that he had approached Golden Harvest Films about making a Tae Kwon Do movie starring Rhee. The opportunity was exciting, but Rhee could scarcely believe it would come to pass—he had never thought of himself as an actor.

Movie poster for Sting of the Dragon Masters with Angela Mao

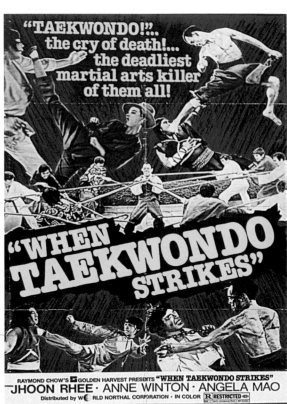

Movie poster for martial arts film, When Tae Kwon Do Strikes

Promotional pictures for When Tae Kwon Do Strikes

Nevertheless, a year later, in the summer of 1973, Rhee flew to Hong Kong to film The Sting of the Dragon Masters, aka When Taekwondo Strikes. In the movie, Rhee plays Grandmaster Lee, the underground leader of a group of patriots in Japanese-occupied Korea. Not only the star of the film, Rhee also wrote the synopsis on which the plot was based.

Jhoon Rhee on location filming When Tae Kwon Do Strikes, 1973

Movie poster for Black Dragon 4

Movie Poster from student Jeff Smith's movie, Return of the Dragon

Production didn't take long; Rhee was back in America by July 19 when Bruce Lee called to say that the movie had been edited and was ready for release. The very next day, Rhee received shocking news: Bruce Lee had passed away. Rhee was one of the last people to talk to the legendary "Little Dragon."

Funeral of Bruce Lee.
Pictured are Steve McQueen, Chuck Norris, Mito Uyehara, and James Coburn

The death of Bruce Lee was devastating for Rhee. He mourned not only the loss of his friend, but the loss to the world of martial arts. Rhee knew that Lee would have continued to make invaluable contributions to the philosophy and influence of their shared passion. So it was with special satisfaction that Rhee was later able to pass along part of Bruce Lee's legacy to one of the greatest athletes of all time, Muhammad Ali.

Rhee first met Ali in 1975, before his "Thrilla in Manila" championship fight with Joe Frazier. Rhee knew that Ali and Bruce Lee never had the chance to meet, so he took the opportunity to show Ali a punch that Rhee had learned from Lee, and for which Rhee had coined a name: the "Accupunch." An extraordinarily fast punch that is almost impossible to block, the Accupunch is based on human reaction time—the idea is to finish the execution of the punch before the opponent can complete the brain-to-wrist communication.

Muhammed Ali with daughter Meme Rhee. Standing - Future Instructor Yoon Lee

Muhammed Ali visiting Korea at Kimpo airport in Seoul after Antonio Inoki fight. There were 1 million spectators.

32

When Rhee demonstrated the punch to Ali, Ali was unable to block it. At Ali's request, Rhee taught him the punch, which he used in his fight against Frazier. Later, Ali also used the Accupunch in a bout with the British champion Richard Dunn—for a knockout blow. During an interview on national TV, a reporter showed Ali a slow-motion replay of the punch and asked about its origin. "That is Mr. Jhoon Rhee's Accupunch," Ali explained. He later elaborated, "I learned the Accupunch from Mr. Jhoon Rhee. It acts at the exact moment you decide to hit, and there is no lag time at all. It is instantaneous. It moves at tremendous speed with no warning and accelerates like a bullet in flight. You can hardly see it."

Jhoon Rhee and Muhammed Ali after Antonio Inoki fight.

Rhee worked as Ali's head coach for both the Dunn fight and for a rare boxing vs. wrestling match in Japan against the famous wrestling champion Inoki. In 1976, Rhee asked Ali to accompany him to South Korea, so its citizens could meet the man who was, at that time, the most popular athlete in the word. When they arrived in June, more than one million people showed up to cheer for Ali in an open-car parade. Rhee and Ali were in Seoul for four days, during which time Ali made more than 12 personal appearances and attended several special events.

Also in 1976, Rhee received a special honor of his own: he was named "Martial Arts Man of the Century" by the Washington Touchdown Sports Club. Comedian Bob Hope was the master of ceremonies at the event, a 2,000-person dinner attended by luminaries including Henry Kissinger, Wilt Chamberlain, and Rhee's friend Muhammad Ali.

Ali Training Center, Deer Lake Pennsylvania

Jhoon Rhee Tae Kwon Do Instructors
in the 1970's

Bottom row left to right: Rodney Batiste, Allan Miller, Jeff Smith, Andre Yamakawa, and Michael Coles. Middle row left to right: Floyd Jackson, Otis Hooper, Larry Curnahan and Howard Chung and on top: Jimmy Rhee and Neil Ehrlich.

Bottom L-R: Howard Chung, Rodney Batiste, Jeff Smith, Jerry Borrows, Bob Barry / Second Row L-R: Neil Erlich, Michael Coles, Dan Magnus, Andre Yumakawa / Third: Danny Bocagno, Dongju Lee, John Chung / Top: Jimmy Rhee, Grand Master Rhee

CHAPTER EIGHT

International Influence (1980 - 2000)

In 1980, Rhee retired from instructing in order to devote his time to expanding his schools and traveling the world to deliver presentations on his Tae Kwon Do philosophy. His first trip, later that year, was a return to South Korea, where Rhee was among the dinner guests for the Presidential inauguration of Chun, Doo-Hwan. As the first person to sign the Blue House guest book, Rhee felt especially honored.

As he spent more time abroad, Rhee's influence in the States continued to grow as well. In 1982, he was requested to serve as the Chairman of our Nation's Fourth of July Birthday Celebration. With the friendships he had made through his U.S. Congressional Tae Kwon Do Club, Rhee was able to organize a prestigious advisory committee consisting of members of the U.S. Senate and House of Representatives. Rhee's signature event for the Celebration was a huge human Stars & Stripes formation, made up of Tae Kwon Do students wearing red, white, and blue uniforms. In the formation, 229 students represented America's population of 229 million; an additional 206 students stood for the 206th Independence Day. The whole group led the Celebration's parade march and later performed "God Bless America" as a martial arts ballet.

Jhoon Rhee Demonstration Team performing the musical ballet God Bless America on the White House lawn, 1983

Although Rhee's personal prominence had reached new heights in America and around the world, the 80s were a time of declining popularity for martial arts in general, at least in the U.S. To counter this, Rhee began a series of martial arts business seminars in 1985 to help struggling school owners across the country, and conducted these monthly seminars for several years.

As Rhee spread his Tae Kwon Do philosophy during this period, he in particular wanted to emphasize the educational benefits of his approach, especially for elementary school children. In the early 80s, with the support of William Bennett, U.S. Secretary of Education during President Reagan's first term, Rhee introduced his "Joy of Discipline" character education program into a couple of DC-area elementary schools, and with the help of Rhee's former student Ken Carlson, later expanded the program into public schools in Virginia.

Rhee also took the program to Moscow and the Ukraine, leading a delegation consisting of eight principals of the DC public school system. While in Moscow, the delegation was joined by 80 Moscow principals for a two-day "Joy of Discipline" program conducted by Rhee.

Master Instructor Inna Krevs head of the Jhoon Rhee
in Moscow with Grand Master Rhee and his wife, Theresa

This turned out to be only the first of several trips to Russia for Rhee. In 1989, he returned to Moscow with several of his students to perform martial arts ballets at an event for both Russian and American dignitaries. During the visit, Rhee also conducted a martial arts philosophy seminar at Moscow University and afterward met with officials of the State Sports Committee to discuss the possible legalization of martial arts as an official Soviet sport. Soon after Rhee's visit, the Committee passed a law legalizing all Asian martial arts activities in the Soviet Union.

Alexander Korobov, director of Jhoon Rhee schools in the former Soviet Union

Rhee returned to Moscow again in 1991 to conduct an 11-day seminar on martial arts philosophy and business practices. At the end of the seminar, 65 of the attending school owners decided to join the Jhoon Rhee system of schools.

The 1991 trip led to Rhee's influence in Russia expanding in a completely unexpected way. At a concert held to conclude and celebrate his seminar, Rhee met the publisher of International Affairs, the official journal of the Soviet Minister of Foreign Affairs, who asked Rhee to write an article for the publication about his philosophy.

In the article, Rhee not only discussed his ideas about martial arts and education, but also his views on the flaws of Soviet communism. After the article's publication, Alexander Potemkin, the Cultural Attaché of the former USSR Embassy in Washington, said: "If you ask me who has now the most influence over the Soviet foreign policies today, I will say it is Master Jhoon Rhee. This editorial article was just published in the Soviet magazine, and read by Soviet diplomats, politicians, and high-level officials. This article consists of guiding principles, the philosophy of Master Rhee, which applies even to relationships between nations and between the Soviet Union and the United States."

Since then, the respect that Rhee is afforded in Russia has only increased; he even received the Russian International Peace Award at a ceremony in Moscow on April 26, 2007.

The international appeal of Rhee's philosophy and success was not limited to Russia. For example, Rhee visited Morocco at the invitation of the government, giving speeches for government agencies, media outlets, and universities. And when Bob Hope retired, Rhee was invited to take over the comedian's famous USO Show in Korea. For two years, in 1999 and 2000, Rhee assembled teams to perform Tae Kwon Do shows for troops in Yongsan and Ohsan.

Of course, Rhee continued to spread his message in America throughout the 80s and 90s, as well.

Jhoon Rhee Independence Day demonstration at the Iwo Jima Memorial, 1991

One of his proudest achievements during this time was National Teacher Appreciation Day. As part of Rhee's commitment to academic and character education for elementary school students, Rhee lobbied 218 lawmakers, most of whom he had met through his Tae Kwon Do classes on the Hill, to establish an official day honoring our nation's teachers. The Honorable E. Clay Shaw of Florida agreed to sponsor the National Teacher Appreciation Day Bill in the U.S. Congress, and on January 28, 1986, it was passed by the House and the Senate. President Reagan signed the bill into law on October 16, 1986.

Jhoon Rhee with former president Ronald Reagan

Jhoon Rhee International Tournament in Washington D.C. with members of his "Congressional Class" and past national champions. Pictured individuals include: Jim Nussle, Dick Sweat, Carmichael Simon, Charlie Lee, John Chung, Tony Lopez, Ishmael Robles, Jeff Smith, Joe Lewis, Pat Worley, Gordon Franks, Nick Smith, Tom Foley, Jhoon Rhee, Jose Santamaria, Mike Espy, Bob Borski

As the end of the century approached, Rhee had accomplished more than he had ever hoped, garnering awards and recognitions almost too numerous to count. He had been named one of President George Bush's Daily Points of Light. His black belt students included not only Members of Congress, but notable figures like Tony Robbins, Jack Valenti, and Jack Anderson. He had appeared on the cover of Parade magazine with Cheryl Tiegs. And he had been named by Black Belt magazine as one of the top two living martial artists of the 20th Century.

Washington DC Fitness Expo - with Carmichael Simon, Francis Pineda, Raffi Kahayan, 1991

Ishamel Robles (right) WKA Title Match, 1981

World Champion
Helen Chung Vasiliadas

Michael Dietrich, World Champion

Jhoon Rhee in front of his home in McLean, VA with his family and colleagues of Muhammad Ali.

Black belt awarded to motivational speaker, Tony Robbins

Asian Chamber of Commerce with Jackie Chan and Susan Allen

Jhoon Rhee forms champion Elsa Cordero

Recent picture with Muhammad Ali

*Jhoon Rhee performing Exodus
at a black belt exam*

Student graduation at Jhoon Rhee, Georgetown, Washington D.C.

Black Belt exam at Jhoon Rhee, Falls Church, VA

Jhoon Rhee Institute, Georgetown, Washington, D.C. location

Students and world champions Jeff Smith and Helen Chung Vasiliadas

CHAPTER NINE

Spreading the Word (2000 - 2018)

Rhee began the new century by adopting new technology, launching jhoonrhee.com in March of 2000 as a way to reach an even larger audience with his philosophy of Tae Kwon Do. Within 45 days, the new website was the world's most popular online martial arts community.

In April of 2000, a month after his arrival on the Internet, Rhee was selected by the National Immigrant Forum, in conjunction with the Immigration and Naturalization Service, as one of the 200 most famous American immigrants of all time, sharing the honor with American icons like Albert Einstein and Knute Rockne. Rhee was the sole immigrant of Korean ancestry to make the list.

In U.S. Representative Nick Smith's Congressional Record Tribute for the honor, he praised Rhee's message as "a philosophy grounded in the principles of the martial arts, but applicable to everyone. It calls for people to build confidence through knowledge in the mind, honesty in the heart, and strength in the body, and then to lead by example."

George Bush, March 29, 2010 - In Houston Office

Three years later, Rhee was also honored by his adopted city, when Mayor Anthony Williams of Washington, DC, declared June 28, 2003 as Jhoon Rhee Day, in commemoration of the founding of the first Jhoon Rhee School on June 28, 1962, and to celebrate the 40th Anniversary of Jhoon Rhee Tae Kwon Do in the Capitol area.

The new century also presented more opportunities for Rhee to share his love of music. He had served as a Board Member of the Washington Symphony Orchestra for several years, and when the Orchestra was deciding on a fundraising event in 2000, Rhee volunteered to perform a Harmonica Concerto in the French Embassy Auditorium. His practice since age six served him well—he used eight different harmonicas of different keys to play Strauss' "Blue Danube." Five years later, the Seoul Royal Symphony Orchestra invited Rhee to join them and perform another Harmonica Concerto, broadcast from the KBS Music Hall.

Korean American Day sponsored by the Korean Economic Institute recognizing Korean Americans in the field of sports. The 2014 inductees were Toby Dawson (Skiing), Jhoon Rhee (Martial Arts), Jim Paek (Ice Hockey), and Hines Ward (Football, not pictured). Former Congressman Donald Manzullo (pictured on the right) is currently the President and CEO of the Korea Economic Institute of America

Instructor Certification - Baltimore, MD

Until 2004, despite Rhee's busy schedule, he maintained an exercise regimen that included both Tae Kwon Do training and 1,000 pushups a day. Then, at age 73, Rhee had to undergo 11 hours of heart surgery. Rhee had been living with a heart murmur since he was born, and during the procedure he suffered a stroke. Still, within two years after the surgery, Rhee was able to break boards again and do 100 pushups in 62 seconds.

Jhoon Rhee Tae Kwon Do, Virginia Tech club started by World Champion Charlie Lee, 1988

Left to right: Myron Adams (in red), Joe Gaydos, Barry Shackelford,
Roger Vasiliadis, Charlie Lee (founder, in black)

Clearly, Rhee is not slowing down. His activities during the last few years include a five-day trip in June of 2007 to Taiwan as State Guests of President Chen, Shui Bien. While there, Rhee gave several speeches to government agencies, universities, and business groups, as well as a private Tae Kwon Do demonstration for the President.

2007 was also the year when Rhee spoke at perhaps his impressive venue yet: the United Nations. Vice Ambassador Joon Oh of the Korean United Nations Mission had heard Rhee speak earlier that year at a Chinese New Year Party for Wall Street dignitaries; he was so impressed with Rhee's message that he invited Rhee to speak at the UN on April 10 before an audience of 200 ambassadors, vice ambassadors, and their staff members. Rhee's speech was entitled, "Mending Our Troubled World through a Philosophy of Action."

Jhoon Rhee with former Russian President, Boris Yeltsen

This same philosophy of action was central to Rhee's message when, two years later, he conducted a five-day conference for OVAL (Our Vision for Asian Leadership) on Jeju Island in 2009. In attendance were about 80 elite university students from Tokyo, Beijing, and Seoul.

Today, Rhee is more committed than ever to a philosophy of action. His message remains consistent with the principles of Tae Kwon Do that have always guided his life, but it has grown much larger, into a way of thought that he believes can not only help each of us lead happier, healthier lives, but also make our world a better place.

It has been more than 80 years since Jhoon Rhee's mother dreamed of a tiger roaring in the jungle. The tiger is still roaring. And still leading by example.

Owners of the newest metro D.C. Jhoon Rhee Tae Kwon Do School, Barry Shackelford and Francis Pineda

Jhoon Rhee was featured on the cover of martial art magazines throughout his career.

Jhoon Rhee's 80th Birthday on Capitol Hill

CHAPTER TEN

Anniversary Banquet

The Jhoon Rhee Insititue 50th Anniversary Banquet and Reunion was hosted at Dennis Brown's U.S. Capitol Classics Tournament on August 3, 2012. The grand event was held at the Gaylord National Resort and Convention Center at National Harbor in Oxon, Maryland just outside of Washington, D.C.

Jhoon Rhee alumni from all over the world were in attendance to honor Grand Master Rhee and to celebrate 50 years of Jhoon Rhee Tae Kwon Do.

Grand Master Rhee was also congratulated by notable friends and colleagues who were unable to attend the event including Muhammad Ali, President George H. W. Bush, Linda Lee Cadwell (widow of Bruce Lee), and others.

Chun Rhee and Meme Rhee

Grand Master Rhee at the Anniversary Celebration

Joe Corley, Michael Coles, Jeff Smith, Walter Anderson, Walter Eddie

Finals show demonstration at U.S. Capitol Classics tournament

Otis Hooper, Barry Shackelford, Charlie Lee

Stephen Oliver, Jhoon Rhee, Michael Coles, Tommy Lightfoot

Helen Chung Vasiliadis, John Chung

Barry Shackelford, Charlie Lee,
Michael Coles, Francis Pineda

Charlie Lee

Larry Carnahan

Francis Pineda presenting congratulatory letter

U.S. Capitol Classics promoter Dennis Brown receiving honorary Jhoon Rhee Black Belt

JHOON RHEE SENIOR INSTRUCTORS

Chun Woo Rhee - Son of Grandmaster Rhee and owner of the Jhoon Rhee Falls Church location. It is the oldest existing school opened in 1974

Barry Shackelford - Co-Owner, Jhoon Rhee Arlington, est 2005

Francis Pineda - Co-Owner, Jhoon Rhee Arlington (right)

Gloria Pereira - Owner, Jhoon Rhee
Hellerstown, PA, est 2005

Mickey Lee, M.Ed. - Co-Owner/Head Instructor,
Georgetown University Tae Kwon Do Club,
(left) est 2001

Melody Lee, M.D., Ph.D. - Co-Owner/Instructor,
Georgetown University Tae Kwon Do Club (right)

Shannon Wong, Master Instructor

Tim Wong, Master Instructor

Fernando Gan, Remote Training Instructor

Black Belt Graduation in Arlington, VA May 2014

*Avi Kalman - Rome, Master Instructor, demonstrates
Jhoon Rhee's 'Belt Stretcher' training tool.*

Manuel Bonilla, Master Instructor

Jackie Curiel, Master Instructor

Deanna Hawk, Senior Instructor

Jace Barrett, Senior Instructor

The magazine cover text (Russian):

ИСКУССТВА ЕВРАЗИИ

спортивно-познавательный журнал

Тулеген Аскеров: Таразский чемпионата JRT • Серик Байтанаев: Очередной приезд отца американского таеквондо Джуна Ри в Алматы. Интервью для журнала "Боевые искусства Евразии" • Антон Воскобойников: Казахстанцы в Малайзии • Нуржан Нургалимов: Тайцзицюань стиль ЯН •

Александр Ли: древнее боевое искусство скифов

Alexander Rhee, Head instructor of Jhoon Rhee Kazakhstan

Jhoon Rhee Seminar in Kazakhstan:
Top Row, left to right - Satybaldyev Asylzhan, Bolganbaeva Alia, Eugene Lee, Kushekbaeva Assel. Bottom Row, left to right - Kaygarodov Igor, Yusupov Askar, Kartabaev Manat, Alexander Rhee, Amenova Kamila, Danil Salimov, Stanislav Ahn, Anatoliy Nee, Sarsenov Zhasulan

2nd World Jhoon Rhee Championship in Almaty Kazakhstan. Pictured left to right – Francis Pineda, Alexander Rhee, Barry Shackelford, Anatoliy Nee

Alexander Korobov, director of Jhoon Rhee schools in the former Soviet Union

Conclusion

When Grandmaster Jhoon Rhee brought Tae Kwon Do to America in 1962, he never imagined that as a teacher of modern martial art he would meet movie stars, sports celebrities, U.S. Congressmen and Senators. He didn't dream of being recognized as an outstanding immigrant or being honored by U.S. Presidents.

Grandmaster Rhee's dream was to introduce you and people just like you to a martial art form that had changed his life. His dream was to help people of all ages strengthen their bodies, enrich their minds and nurture their hearts.

As we celebrate a half-century of Tae Kwon Do in America Grandmaster Rhee wishes to say, "Thank You" for helping his dream to come true in ways he never thought imaginable, and for carrying in your hearts the desire to develop "Might For Right."

The Jhoon Rhee Institute "Student Creed"

"To build true confidence through Strength in my Body,
Honesty in my Heart, and Knowledge in my Mind.
To keep friendship with one another and
to build a Strong and Happy community.
Never fight to achieve selfish ends,
but to develop Might For Right!"

ACKNOWLEDGEMENTS

We would like to recognize the following people for their generous contributions toward this book:

- Former Congressman Bob Livingston
- Walter Anderson
- Kamil Landa
- Dongju Lee
- John Simpson
- Grace and Mike Hodges
- Barry and Heather Shackelford
- Francis and Elizabeth Pineda

DEATH & MEMORIAL SERVICE

Grandmaster Jhoon Rhee passed away on April 30, 2018. He had suffered years of pain from neuralgia due to the shingles virus. He was 86 years old. At his memorial service, hundreds of martial artists gathered in their martial arts uniforms to pay their respects to the man who brought Tae Kwon Do to the United States, championed knowledge, honesty and strength, and always led by example.

Also in attendance were politicians Toby Roth, Connie Morella, Jesse Jackson, Jesse Jackson, Jr. and others. Speaking or providing video tributes were politicians, actors and other dignitaries such as Linda Lee Cadwell (the widow of Bruce Lee), Chuck Norris, Allen Steen (his first student), Tony Robbins (student), Iain Armitage (student), former Speaker of the House Bob Livingston, U.S. Secretary of Transportation Elaine Chao, Speaker of the House Paul Ryan, former Virginia Governor George Allen, Maryland Governor Larry Hogan, and other notables. *(See the following memorial service program for a complete list of those sharing remembrances at the service.)*

Memorial placed at Jhoon Rhee's gravesite in Falls Church, VA

It was estimated that over the 50 years that Grandmaster Rhee headed the Jhoon Rhee Institute he or his instructors promoted over 100,000 Black Belts. This is an incredible legacy. As his son, Chun Rhee, stated in closing the Memorial Service: "In 50 years just imagine what one person did... just imagine what 100,000 could do in the next 50. So when you leave here today, love what you do, and know that your job as a martial arts instructor is important. So I ask that we all stand, for one last bow...'Class, Charyot, Kyong ye!'"

— *Celebrating* —
the LIFE AND LEGACY of

GRANDMASTER

Jhoon Rhee

Tuesday, May 8, 2018

MCLEAN BIBLE CHURCH | VIENNA, VIRGINIA

Order of Service

11:00AM	**WELCOME** *Introduction of the Family*	Jimmy Rhee/Chun Rhee *Sons*
11:10 AM	**SCRIPTURE READING**	Rev. Nathan Crew *McLean Bible Church*
11:15 AM	**JHOON RHEE - THE FATHER OF U.S. TAE KWON DO** SPECIAL TRIBUTES *Linda Lee Cadwell* *Widow of Martial Arts Legend Bruce Lee & Friend* *Chuck Norris* *Martial Artist, Actor, & Friend* *Musical Ballet Tribute* *The Departure by Michael Nyman*	Jimmy Rhee *Son* Rasta Thomas *Internationally Renowned Dancer,* *Choreographer, & Jhoon Rhee Student*
11:40 AM	**PRAYER FOR FAMILY AND SERMON**	Rev. Nathan Crew *McLean Bible Church*
11:50 PM	**TRIBUTES (Video)** *Tony Robbins* *Author, Philanthropist, Life Coach, &* *Jhoon Rhee Black Belt* *Ernie Reyes Sr.* *Master, Co-founder & Head Instructor* *of West Coast World Martial Arts* *Iain Armitage* *Actor (Young Sheldon) & Jhoon Rhee Student* *Paul Ryan* *U.S. Speaker of the House* *Elaine Chao* *U.S. Secretary of Transportation* *Larry Hogan* *Governor of Maryland*	Jimmy Rhee *Son*

12:10 PM	**TRIBUTES** *Eun Gil Choi* *Chairman, U.S. TKD & Martial Arts* *Grandmasters Federation* *Bob Livingston* *Former Speaker of the House-Elect*	Jimmy Rhee *Son*
12:20 PM	**AMAZING GRACE** *Harmonica Musical Tribute*	Sam Rhee *Grandmaster Rhee's* *Younger Brother*
12:25 PM	**TRIBUTES** *Allen Steen* *Grandmaster Rhee's First Black Belt Student* *Michael Coles* *Master, Former Jhoon Rhee Head Instructor* *Jeff Smith* *Master, Former Jhoon Rhee Instructor &* *PKA World Champion*	
12:35 PM	**NEARER MY GOD TO THEE** *Traditional Hymn*	Lena Seikaly *Vocalist & Jhoon Rhee* *Black Belt*
12:40 PM	**TRIBUTES** *Charlie Lee* *Former Jhoon Rhee Instructor & Family Friend* *Meme Rhee* *Youngest Daughter of Grandmaster Rhee*	
12:50 PM	**GOD BLESS AMERICA** *Martial Arts Ballet*	Francis Pineda & Jhoon Rhee Demo Team
12:55 PM	**BENEDICTION**	Rev. Kenneth Carlson *International Calvary Church*
1:00 PM	**FINAL BOW TO GRANDMASTER RHEE**	Chun Rhee *Son*

RECEPTION AND LIGHT REFRESHMENTS IN THE LOBBY

*The Rhee Family expresses their
deep gratitude in sharing
his life and legacy.*

LIVE IN
TRUTH, BEAUTY, AND LOVE

—Jhoon Rhee

Memorial services orchestrated by Lisa Lee, Daughter-in-Law.

Program designed by Kimberly Rhee, Granddaughter.

And, THANK YOU to all volunteers…